Gemma Hunt's
SEE! LET'S BE

For my Gracious One
and my Bringer of Joy
and Blessing.

You're my FAVOURITES.

G.H x

For my Songbird, my
Treasure Bringer, and
the glue that keeps me
together. I love you.

Cl xxx

Gemma Hunt's
SEE! LET'S BE
A Good Friend

illustrated by Charlotte Cooke

LION
Children's Books

Published by **Lion Children's Books**
www.lionhudson.com
Part of the SPCK Group
SPCK, 36 Causton Street, London, SW1P 4ST

ISBN 978 0 7459 7951 9

First edition 2022

A catalogue record for this book is available from the British Library

Printed and bound in China, January 22, LH54

Our dear Mr Preston,
May you grow to be a loving, sharing, kind, selfless and helpful boy, who always knows how loved he is!

With our love,
Amy, John, Zach & Levi
x o x o

Contents

Love

I'm **sad**. My best-loved cuddly has **gone**.

He is a rabbit, called Babbit, with long white ears and a worn nose where I **snuggle** him at bedtime.

I **love** my Babbit. And now he isn't here.
He's important to me so I **need** to find him.

Where **could** he be?
Behind my bed? **No**.
In my wardrobe? No.
In the kitchen? **No**.
In my book bag? No.

In a cupboard? A basket? A box of puzzles? **No**.

Maybe he is hiding like the sheep the farmer lost.

The farmer was sad **too**. He looked around the field and **couldn't** find the missing sheep.

He looked in the sheep pen but **couldn't** find it.

Love

He looked around the farmhouse,
the allotment, the yard, **and** the pond,
but **couldn't** find it.

Love

It was breakfast time for the sheep and they were **all** hungry and bleating **loudly**, but he **couldn't** feed them until he found the **lost** sheep.

Love

He sat down on a bench,
beside the barn, to think
where it might be. **Suddenly**, he
felt a **wriggle** underneath him.

IT WAS THE SHEEP!

The little lamb was lost and had **hidden**,
scared and shaking, **under** the bench.

The farmer was **so** happy to find it that he **scooped** the sheep up, gave it a huge **cuddle**, and ran back to the field with it on sheepyback — because sheep don't do piggybacks!

Love

Now *everyone* was **happy**. The little lost sheep was back with its family, the farmer had **all** his sheep again, and now they could **ALL** enjoy breakfast together.

I still hadn't found Babbit when it came to dinner time. All **day** I had looked for him. I **couldn't** eat my spaghetti, I was too **sad**.

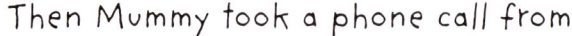

Then Mummy took a phone call from a friend who was **stuck** at the train station in the rain and needed a lift home.

Mummy is **very** loving and said we would come **straight** away. We had to leave our spaghetti to go and collect her, but as I put my wellies on, guess who I found? **Babbit!** Hiding! I was **so** happy to find him.

He looked after my spaghetti until we got back home and Mummy warmed it up for me. It was **so** yummy in my tummy and my heart was **happy** too.

Love

Share

Share. **Share** your toys, but they're my toys.

Share. **Share** your sweets, but they're my sweets.

Share. **Share** your seat, but it's my seat – I was here **first!**

Share. Share. SHARE!

I **keep** hearing this, but I **don't** want to have less.

Why do I have to share something if it is **MINE?** I got it first. It was given to **me.** I like it. I **want** it. It's **mine.** Maybe I should be **more** like the boy who had a very cool lunch box.

The boy's lunch box was **bright** orange and had a picture of a funny face on it.
When you moved it, the eyes went all **goggly**, and the handle was its hair, all green and **spiky**.
It looked funny.

Inside he had **two** tuna sandwiches and **five** big breadsticks.

He was asked to **share** his lunch with a **big** crowd of people who were at a picnic but had **FORGOTTEN** to pack **their** lunch! That seemed **silly**. Why go to a picnic and not take **anything** to eat?

Guess what he was asked to **do** with his lunch? Yep — share.

"Share your sandwiches, dear," said a lady whose tummy was rumbling.

"Break up your breadsticks and share them out," said a man who looked **tired** and hungry.

The boy held his orange lunch box close
to his chest as another man came over
and said that if **he** could share his lunch,
everyone there could eat.

Share

The man **held** out his hand, and the boy **gave** him the orange lunch box.

The goggly eyes wiggled as the man **opened** the box and handed out the food to his friends, who shared it with everyone. *EVERYONE!*

Share

They **all** ate, which made their tummies full and their hearts happy. They **even** had lots left to take **home** for the next day.

Share

Wow! That was amazing. Maybe I should share my things when others have nothing?

Mummy's friend came to visit yesterday and said she was going to a party and didn't have **anything** to wear. Mummy said she could borrow a new dress she had been given — that's Mummy sharing too. Her friend was **so** happy to have something new to wear to the party.

So, even grown-ups share! I'm going to try harder to share my things, like my sweets. My tummy might not be **so** full, but we will all be happy.

Kindness

The man next door is **grumpy**.

If I play music too loud, he bangs on the walls.

If I **kick** a ball over the fence, he won't let me have it back.

He complains if we **don't** mow our lawn.

When it's recycling day, he rolls his noisy bin out so early that it wakes up the dog down the street, who starts **barking** loudly. And then he **moans** at the dog.

After the bins have been emptied, he's the first one out to put his bin away.

My dad always pushes everyone's bins back down their driveway after the recycling men have been and I like to **wave** at them. But the man next door doesn't want to be part of **our** community.

He's a bit like the **grumpy** boy at school.

At lunch time, he **bashes**
around the lunch hall
taking snacks and drinks
from people and then sits
at a table by **himself**
to **eat** it all.

He **already** has his own packed lunch but takes things that aren't his from other people.

No one wants to sit with him, **so** he only has his **stolen** food to keep him company.

But then **one day** last week, a new girl started, who was **smiley** and kind and nice. Lots of people went up to her and **laughed** and **talked** and shared lunch with her.

And **then** something very unusual happened: she sat on the grumpy boy's table! She is the **FIRST** person I've seen **sit** with him to eat lunch. She just sat there and chatted to him. She **smiled**, and then he **smiled** too!

Kindness

Now each lunch time he brings in **extra** food to **share** with everyone, and we **all** want to sit on his table!

Kindness

I wanted to do something kind for the man next door.

Even though he is grumpy, I know he is a good man and maybe an act of **kindness** might make him smile.

So **today**, it was sunny, and I heard the ice cream man driving into our street.

I **took** some money from my piggy bank and asked Dad **if** I could **spend** it on an ice cream. He said I could, so I bought two little ones, one for **me** and **one** for the man **next door**.

When I handed it to him, he smiled **SO** brightly like the sun that I thought our ice creams were going to melt!

Selflessness

I love staying with my Nana and **her** cats. They're great!
In the mornings I can watch all the shows I love on her **big** TV
and eat lots of **yummy** cereal from her big bowls. She has SO
much choice of cereal! I know which is her **best one**, as it is
my best one **too**.

So, I pour a BIG bowl for **myself** and finish it off.

Lulu the tabby cat **plays** with the box.

Nana comes to sit down and **reaches** for the box.

"Oh!" she says. "It's empty! I don't remember finishing this."

I've got a yucky feeling in my **tummy**, like the cereal I've just
eaten wants to come out and scream... so I cry out.
"Nana, I ate it! Sorry, it was so yummy, I just had to have it."
Nana looked sad. **"Look** at Lulu," she said.

When Lulu came to me, she was **thin** and
quiet and scared because the cats
she used to live with were **mean** to her.

My cats were not so nice to her at first either. Mia would **scratch** her if she went near the milk.

Bluebell wouldn't let her eat any food.
They were **selfish**, just thinking
of themselves.

Selflessness

But Dinky — he has been **kind**.
He **moved** out of his cat bed to let Lulu
get comfy and pushed his toy mouse
toward her with his paw.

Selflessness

He was selfless — he loved Lulu and put her first, **even** though she **wasn't** his friend.

Now look at how **happily** they **play** together!

Nana sat me on her lap and **whispered** sweetly in my ear as we **watched** the cats playing.

"Now, my love, when you do things, don't let selfishness tell you what to do. Instead, **think** about others as being more important than yourself and this will make you and them feel much happier."

Nana was **so** kind — she didn't get upset, she didn't shout.
She was showing me how she was being **selfless**,
putting **ME** and my greedy tummy before herself.

This made me love her **even** more and want to do something
nice for her.

So, I got all the cereals, mixed up lots of **yummy** ones together,
and put them in a **big** special bowl.

I turned the TV over to the show
she loves and cuddled up next
to her. It **feels** good to do something
kind for someone, and nice to sit next
to that **special** person while
she enjoys her breakfast.

Helpfulness

"It's party time," smiled Mum, **twirling** balloons on ribbons around her head.

"Let's **bake** the cake," said Dad, grabbing his apron and trying to **juggle** eggs.

"Granddad's birthday," laughed my little sister as she **danced** around in circles getting **dizzy**.

I love my Granddad — he **builds** dens with us, **fixes** our bikes, and makes yummy pancakes. But **all** I can hear are **my** friends outside **kicking** a ball around and I want to be out there with **them**, not inside setting up a **party** for the family.

I **pick** up a balloon and **drop-kick** it, like Coach showed us last week at training. It bounces off my prize trophy that my team and I **won** at our last match. That was a great day.

We had our new kit on — **bright** purple
and white, with shining black boots.

Helpfulness

We played our **best** game
EVER! I scored **twice** and
the crowds cheered so loud
I thought my **big grin** would
fall off my face!

Helpfulness

When *we* **lifted** the trophy,
Coach looked so **proud**.
He **wouldn't** say so, but I think
he had a little tear in his eye.

After the game, we **celebrated** with hotdogs and milkshakes.

But when it was time for Coach to give a speech, he was nowhere to be seen.

I looked on the pitch — **not there.**

In the café — **not there.**

In the changing room, not there...
or so I thought.

I could see all our muddy boots piled up and Coach sitting behind them lovingly cleaning them up ready for the next match.

What a guy! After **helping** us win, he missed the celebrations to do **ALL** the tidying up.

Coach is my hero. His **help** meant so much to our team.

Maybe I should be more like him and be a **good** team player in my family now to **help** finish off the party preparations. I picked up the balloon and drew a big smiley face on it, with a beard, moustache, and glasses.

It **looked** just like Granddad!

I took it to the kitchen and called out, "Where's the cake? I'll help put the candles on."

Dad passed me the candles and put my balloon next to the cake.

Now the party was ready!

When Granddad arrived, we all cheered,
"Happy Birthday, Granddad — we love you!"

He was so pleased, his moustache wiggled as he smiled the biggest smile. He loved us all being there together. My sister and I helped him blow out the candles and I handed around the cake, as **everyone** enjoyed this special family party.

The stories in this book have been inspired by these Bible stories:

Love

The parable of the lost sheep

Luke 15:3–7

Share

The feeding of the 5,000

John 6:1—14

Kindness

Jesus meets Zacchaeus

Luke 19:1—10

Selflessness

The parable of the good Samaritan
Luke 10:25–37

Helpfulness

Jesus washes his disciples' feet

John 13:1–17

"Gemma has done a lovely job of bringing to life
the teachings of Jesus for the everyday experience
of children and their families."

Bob Hartman
Storyteller and award-winning author